EROS, UNBROKEN

Also by Annie Kim:

Into the Cyclorama

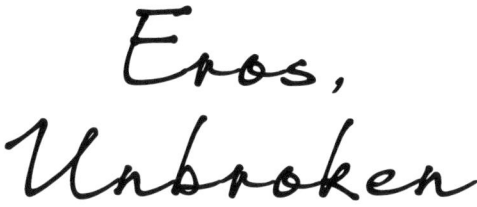

ANNIE KIM

WINNER OF THE 2019 WASHINGTON PRIZE
Andrea Carter Brown, Series Editor

THE WORD WORKS
WASHINGTON, D. C.

Eros, Unbroken © 2020 Annie Kim

Reproduction of any part of this book in any form or by any means, electronic or mechanical, except when quoted in part for the purpose of review, must be with permission in writing from the publisher. Address inquiries to:

The Word Works
P.O. Box 42164
Washington, D.C. 20015
editor@wordworksbooks.org

Cover art: Lucas Cranach the Elder,
"Judith with the Head of Holofernes," ca. 1530
Courtesy of the Open Access Collection
of the Metropolitan Museum of Art
Cover design: Susan Pearce Design
Author photograph: Annie Kim

ISBN: 978-1-944585-37-2

Acknowledgments

Grateful acknowledgment is made to the journals in which the following poems appear, often in different form:

Beloit Poetry Journal: "A Hysteresis Loop."

The Cincinnati Review: "Eros the Binder and Loosener" and "Eros the Contagion."

Four Way Review: "Violins: Violence" and an earlier version of "Castrato" and "Castrato ("desire must *vary*")."

Mudlark: "Confession," "Uses for Music," "Dear Riccardo," "Dear Riccardo (II)," "Everything Swims," "Fire Chasing Air," "To Hold Something Close," and "Bright Skin of a Snake."

Narrative: "Bildungsroman, 1999."

Pleiades: "Breaking Up with Eros."

Plume: "Post-."

Plume Anthology, Vol. 8: "The Hydrangeas."

Contents

Confession • 11

ONE

Eros the Binder and Loosener • 17
Friend • 18
Violins: Violence • 19

TWO

Castrato • 31
Girl Changing Shape • 36
Castrato ("desire must *vary*") • 37

THREE

A Hysteresis Loop • 43
Ghost • 50

FOUR

Uses for Music • 53
Dear Riccardo • 54
Eros the Hunter • 56
Dear Riccardo, (II) • 57
Everything Swims • 58
Soft • 61
Fire Chasing Air • 63
Bildungsroman, 1999 • 65
To Hold Something Close • 66
Breaking Up with Eros • 67

FIVE

    The Hydrangeas • 71
    Post- • 76
    Bright Skin of a Snake • 77
    Another Sonata • 80
    Eros the Contagion • 84
    Leap • 85
    The Thief Dreams • 86

NOTES • 89

About the Author / Thanks • 91
About The Word Works • 92
Other Word Works Books • 93

for all my loves, especially my husband

Confession

The book in the library was yellow like the sun in a fraying tapestry. Titled simply: *Domenico Scarlatti*. I took it to an alcove where morning light streamed in through the picture window behind me, opened to the flyleaf, and read.

•

Story: a thing tangled up with something else. *Eros*: what tangles them.

•

What I wanted on that clear summer morning was not biography, but passion. To dive like a small blue whale into the ocean. The hunt is rarely about the thing.

•

Scarlatti: composer son of a famous composer, whose more than 550 keyboard sonatas, largely unpublished at his death in 1757, are the music of a divided self. Father. Gambler. Bankrupt.

Castrato: one who cuts his body to preserve his voice.

Farinelli: castrato singer, the most celebrated in all of Europe, Scarlatti's friend. Who quit the opera stage to sing each night to mad Philip V of Spain. Whose body, like Saint Sebastian's in the Bernini sculpture that I love, twists even as it's pierced.

•

To be a thief you must love what you steal. I saw that I could write myself into their shadows. That I would need to pierce myself.

•

Counterpoint: the art of building by pursuing more than one melodic line, each independent but connected to the other.

> [Eros] is not form-giving but form-fulfilling; it is the wine that will be poured into the vessel; it is not the bed and direction of the stream but the impetuous water flowing in it.
>
> —Carl Jung, *Liber Novus*, App. B, 56

ONE

Eros the Binder and Loosener

There was a black reflecting pool in the center of the garden.

Guarding it, a pair of lion statues at the top of the steps, looking down.
Pink azaleas gone frothy by the pool's edge, then tiers of boxwood, pines—

I know because of the photographs, my attempts to *take*.

Something in the water let it be both black and reflective.
Staring into it, almost touching the glossy surface, all I could see was water:
no sign of my hovering face, only depthless, witchy satin.

But everything far away? All of it was held there, no loss of color or shape.
And when the wind shook the tall pines, their image in the water shook.

Speaking to my ghost tonight, her face half in shadow, her voice
slipping unevenly down the rocks, how easy I feel it is
to fall in, how dark and sweet this water is, all the light it contains.

Friend

Come, she said, *I want to show you
a black snake*. Sun glaring hot
on the bleached white gravel.

Come, she said, *it isn't dangerous*—
and so I dumbly followed.
Don't want to see the head, I
could've said, but then I saw it—
no bigger than my thumb.

Don't want to see all black, I
might've thought, but then it wasn't:
cream along the belly. Soft.

Friend, I want to ask it,
how did you come into the open?

Violins: Violence

Vitula. Viol. Violino.
             Violare. Violentus. Violentia.

"Origin and History of Violence," reads the header.

You've visited this page 3 times.

•

Last night you dreamed again
about your father—

You had him by the wrists:
above your head, the way you'd catch
a snake, one hand beneath
its flickering tongue,

             fighting hard to not
get bitten (you've worked so hard
to not get bitten),
other hand wrestling with the slick,
elusive tail—

•

Violins: Violence. No shared root for these words, but isn't it interesting that the Japanese counter word (*cho*) for violins includes *scissors, gun* and *rickshaw*? As in, Give me a *cho* of violins. And some guns.

Vitulare—to "sing or rejoice"—is related to *vitula*, deity of victory, thanks-giving, and Roman festivals, giving us the root for *fiddle* and *violin*. *Vitula* (also "calf"), because calf guts were used for violin strings.

•

Morning: the dream has left the bed.

        Your chest feels like
batting in a pillow, no upholstery,
no fringe. Behind the wall,
water splashes the bathtub tiles,
your husband's whistling—

        Mahler-something, each space
between his cheerfully constructed
notes absolute. Yes,

your father hurt you. Loved,
in fact, to hurt you
so all the hurt could flee the burning
forests in his body, slither out to
enter yours, renewed—

he could see for a moment then
shapes he couldn't bear to watch alone,
a man bending down in the dark
to blow out a crown of birthday candles.

Then everything would be sweet again.
You could eat the cake because
sweet is what your body craved.

•

Violare looks a lot like *vitulare*, but it means to violate, to wrong.

        In my old life I argued to a judge that the definition of *wrongful act* includes *violations* of pre-existing *duty*, that loss includes claims for *liquidated damages*. I lost. Not all bad acts are wrongful acts, he said. Not all loss is bargained for.

•

Standing in the shower, you feel a lump
on your scalp, behind the ear.
How did it get there? Can't

remember, but that feeling—

something swollen, buried
beneath your dripping hair—

is familiar. Almost comforting.

Like a picture that you've seen
a thousand times on a billboard
appearing on your phone screen—
crisp, so crisp.

•

                          You remember
little things: his white
Hanes undershirt, fingers
small and meticulous, working
the potato peeler—

                swivel of those long,
jack-o'-lantern-orange strips

he scraped from the carrot falling,
julienned, on the open paper.

How they soaked the newsprint.

•

Shit-like offspring—

that was his favorite
curse for you in Korean.
It had a satisfying ring:
dactyl plus a trochee;
five hard consonants.

Some days it was *dog offspring*.
When he was feeling, say,
less creative, just *bad offspring*.

•

                                              Done trying
whatever names he had for you,
he'd pick up the bleeding newspaper,
dump the peels into the trashcan—
tap tap against the molded plastic.

Flick the last few strips
with his pearly nail tip.

•

Quote from Marcus Aurelius, Book II of the *Meditations*:

    "When you wake up in the morning, tell yourself: The people I will deal with today will be meddling, ungrateful, arrogant, dishonest, jealous, and surly. They are like this because they can't tell good from evil."

Tell yourself what cures
is the power of discrimination—

        that was *child* you, not *now*

you, writing this—

If you know you were wronged, who was wrong,
well, shouldn't you be okay?

       •

        Sound from a violin (what we call music) is the product

   of a chain of fine aggressions and reactions: draw the *bow*

        slung with stiff white horsehair (only horses that have lived

in cold weather countries) across four strings (sheep-gut core

        wound in silver or aluminum), start a tremor in the *bridge*

carved from unbleached maple beneath the strings, sending ripples

        to the *soundpost* (spruce) lodged upright in the belly—

       •

        You feel fat and sad.

        Is this because
        of him, what he did to you (*to*
        you)? Is that the right

        preposition?

                                        You want to smash

                              something. Thumbnail
                              digging into nail bed, your hands
                              slack on the wheel. What have you

                              smashed, ever?

                                        •

Standing over you: he. The hand

                              (or is it fist?)

slamming the side of (why
are you recalling

                              this?) the head. Yours.

Face turned. There is
                              no clarity,

I'm done with you!

                              no single instant—

only reel, only the girl

                              going down, getting up, go-
ing down:

                              endless loop, bad audio.

A few seconds.

•

—Make the *soundpost* ring. That's what it's built for:

flood on flood of quick vibrations. Make it tremble,
make it echo every note you play, transmit

like a good little messenger every wave to the silent
forests of the body, out again

through two holes in the belly's surface, called *f-holes*.
As in the italic letter *f*, since only holes

release music from an instrument. As in *forte, fine, fuck*.

•

>   You want to smash something.
>   Instead, you sing along
>   to the radio—

>   *On the long way down,*
> *Oh oh oh, oh oh oh—*

>   feel the seizing in your gut,

>   how it tightens then
>   lets go.

>   Stop for the school bus flashing red.
>   Tick-tock, tick-tock.

•

Marcus Aurelius continues:

"But I have seen the beauty of good, and the ugliness of evil, and have recognized that the wrongdoer has a nature related to my own—not of the same blood or birth, but the same mind, and possessing a share of the divine. *And so none of them can hurt me.*"

•

O beauty of her bathroom, patience of the door that shields her
from the brittle house of him. O mirror in the cabinet never
filled with medicine, bulbs in the fixture always electric. O head,
a ball of playdough abandoned on the blacktop in the pouring
summer rain, water in the holes dug by a pencil. O trace
for which she searches half in horror, half in vain, of her father's
latest handprint—proof of what the fire did, what beams
of the cathedral look like burned. Camera, are you getting this?

Take the roof off this house, spot the hallway to the narrow
master bathroom where he sits. Show us the newspaper:
pages falling open on his knees with a sound like a fan
clicking shut or clicking open, sooty wings of an angel neither
good nor evil, just a messenger. O beauty of believing in
the sweet independence of things: coldness of the washcloth lifted
to her head, water in the sink, pacing of her mother in the kitchen.
O sanity in thinking even she (little weakling thing)
could at this moment, if she chose to, simply hate him.

•

I won my appeal.

When I read *reversed*, I jumped up in my empty office, yelling, "Suck it, Judge _____ ! I rejoiced and sang, I'd never felt so victorious.

•

"No one can implicate me in ugliness. Nor can I feel angry at my relative, or hate him."

Oh, Marcus.

TWO

Tell me, what would you do for a perfect voice?

Tell me what perfection means to you.
Completion? Rapture? Pain?

Castrato

I want to be a boy, you tell the man
who analyzes you. *Free of desire.*

He nods, light flashing
off his thin gold spectacles.

                              No one called the singing boys
                              castrati to their face. So *evirato*,
                              meaning one unmanned,
                              musico: one making music.

Boys aren't free
of desire, of course—

                              Though not by ordinary means—
                              fingers pressing keyboard, lips
                              against a cold silver mouthpiece.
                              No, the singer's body turned
                              to supple balsam, stretched
                              over the years until it forms
                              that frame beloved by engineers—
                              strength, endurance, range—

You uncross your legs, recross:
left over right. Beneath you
the vintage leather cushion sinks.

It's the idea that they aren't
committed yet.

                              until those sheer, adolescent ribs
                              ascend like arches in a nave, not merely
                              the idea of being holy, no—
                              the blood and the meat. Only then
                              is the sacrifice complete.

Out the window a crane lifts;
staccato drilling.

    I'm sorry,
the man says, waving—
all this construction.

It seems appropriate, you say.

          Only then will the whole frame sing.
          Become a building large enough
          to contain the singer's longing—
          all his longing, all our own—

But no, what you told him
wasn't true—

    what you want
is to feel *everything*, desire
as the scarlet tape beneath
clear casing, what you

want is not the package, solid
in your hands, but
pleasure in the pulling,
ripping off the plastic.

          enough to let us watch him
          grow transparent: liquid, dim
          in the dusk as a cool glass bowl.

          And who are we to question, we
          who bend our ears to listen?

•

Violare, you tell the man
who analyzes you,

                            is a beautiful word
despite its meaning.

Unlike *victim*, unlike *vulnerable*.

Castration was never, strictly speaking, desirable. Or legal.

But beauty made the mutilation worthy. Money made it prudent. So *castrati* trained to sing like angels performed God's masses, played the parts of men and women—lovers, heroes, villains—in the candelabraed courts of kings and queens. Got rich as rock stars. Were beloved.

I became enamoured of *castrati*. One they called "the boy" at first—*Il Ragazzo* in Italian—then Farinelli, after a pair of bankers who were his patrons. Born Carlo Maria Michelangelo Nicola Broschi, though no one called him that. A friend of the composer Domenico Scarlatti, though no double portrait of the two exists.

Late summer: listening to a sonata by Scarlatti recorded on piano, bristling with needle-like precision. What I can tell you is it *jumped*. Scarlatti jumped. Off the tracks into unrelenting dirt, showing us a glimpse of his mind, that private dark plummet we hide from ourselves, from others, every day.

Then up again: perfect sun, remorseless summer green of trees.

            You've been abused, he says slowly,
            taking care to look into your eyes.

                        Mind (*your* mind)
            jumps, a slapped animal. Blink,
            twitch—

            I hate that word,
            you begin,

            I don't want to think of myself
            as a victim. Tight, your smile.

                    •

don't look afraid   don't hit back

(that only

       makes it worse)

talking about it   makes it worse

      say as little as possible

                    •

Snap as the bridge
collapses, soundpost

slips from its perfect,
upright posture, tumbling

through the empty
wooden torso, little dowel

whose only duty is
to echo (are we doomed

to echo?) every wave that
slaps it through your hungry violin—

one thing making
another sing, because there is

no music without violence,
no song unless a chain.

And when the tumbling stops?

In your hands a newly
metamorphosed box.

Girl Changing Shape

"And she would easily escape: she'd take shape after shape..."
—Ovid, *Metamorphoses*, Book VIII

Girl in this instant, man

        breaking into her

ocean, the man parting

        her weak thighs a god.

You see, the ocean needs

        a face; rupture, cause—

he's not just fucking her.

        No, she's no victim.

It's the *ocean* smearing

        salt on her thighs, girl
        spitting, gasping, flap-

ping like a beached fish, dropping

        like a cold stone, dropped.

Then stroking her wet cheek,

        bending to whisper—

Now my power is yours.

Castrato ("desire must vary")

—In the voice of Carlo Broschi.
Naples, 1710s.

No one speaks the words. Silent at the table,
four of us now, a new boy clearing dishes,
first the plates—the ones Father bought in London—
then the knives and forks. The big clock strikes ten,
still Mother doesn't say, Carlo, time for bed.
Riccardo, at the head of the table—
barely a week since Father passed away—
sitting high and black as a graveyard gate,
Sofie twisting day-old daisies in her lap.
The estate, Riccardo says. *Decisions*.
Mother creasing her black lace handkerchief.
A pair of bankers, he begins slowly,
brothers. They have heard of Carlo's talents.
The large fruit bowl remains on the table,
Father's favorite—a pair of ladies dancing,
fingers hidden in their fluttering sleeves—
two oranges huddled inside it, mute.
They believe his debut would be brilliant.

"At the origin of Narrative,"
Roland Barthes writes in *S/Z*,

"desire."

Sometimes you hear the frozen river split
and yet you step onto the ice—I ask,
When can it be done, this thing? Can it be soon?
Mother staring deep into her handkerchief,
as if there is an answer there, a stitch
she can unravel with the needle's tip.
No one makes us plunge into the river:

                we walk because there is no standing still.
                    Then Riccardo, O you whom I adore,
                 how you turned to me and, smiling, said:
                       Little brother, let it be as you wish.
                 I will call on the brothers Farinello.

       Desire in the text
beneath the text—

Barthes writing about a tale by Balzac,
a castrato singer, baffling
as the object of desire.
Though he's writing about himself.

       (You can only tell
this tale through indirection.)

                Rain. Rain. A few drops cling to the window,
                   drop without a sound to the sill. Wet wind
                      blowing in: it barely touches me. Please,
let no one touch me. Just this bed, this bandage
        wrapped around my shattered mast like a sail,
            the nightshirt I refuse to let them change.
        Mother's footsteps in the hall. Then her head
        bent over like the Virgin. Prayers. A candle.
       We're sailing, I'm sure of it—I'm seasick,
          gagging again and again into a basin—
      a hand wipes my head with a cold wet towel.

"To produce narrative, however,
desire must *vary*, must enter into a system
of equivalents and metonymies . . ."

> I am winding through a stonewalled garden.
> Someone mowed the grass. The clover's headless,
> dew soaks my feet, my night shirt is too thin—
> If only I can find the door I'll find him
> sitting on the bench he loved, composing,
> whole again: Father in the shade of a tree.
> *A ritornello, son. You will sing it soon.*
> He lifts up the manuscript, freshly inked—
> a simple tune, andante. Just a scale
> branching out like a tree designed to branch,
> until it doesn't, snapped without a reason.
> Silence in the cooling air. Now it's dusk.
> Father looking up at me from shadows:
> *Son, what are you holding in your fist?*

You have always seen yourself
as strong—discipline

your muscles, rid
your body of itself.

> Daylight. Nothing in the mirror has changed.
> One lock of hair, still damp, slides down my head—
> push it back. We must be perfect, he and I,
> perfectly natural, calm, and gracious.
> I move my lips: he smiles back instantly,
> as if he's worried I will find him out,
> crying and clinging to the post of his bed.
> *Everything looks the same*, I whisper to him.
> *My voice. Nothing will happen to my voice.*
> He is silent. In the depths of his eyes
> a flash—silver, something twitching—a fish?
> Tiny, iridescent. Fire in the pool.

Your never-needing, never-
weakling self your mask.

Until now, impeccable.

>Twilight: Mother spoons honey in my tea.
>Alone in my room, one window open.
>*You're just a boy*, she croons.
>Though we both know
>that's the point—this hole we'll never speak of,
>my softness like a fruit. When all the other
>glass bells smash, only I will stay unbroken.
>A boy. Always a boy. *Il Ragazzo.*
>Farinelli.

THREE

A Hysteresis Loop

For any phenomenon there is a shape—dashed lines, points in a plot.

: a loop, say a fountain pen's italic *f*.

I want to tell you that it's beautiful.

•

        Sir James Alfred Ewing, studying earthquakes in Tokyo—it was the Meiji era, late 1880s, Brahms hard at work on his third piano trio—discovered that magnetic force, when applied to pianoforte wire, both saturates and flees the wire at the same rate, creating a mirror image over time, chartable over time. There was a lag, however, between cause and effect.

He named this *hysteresis*.

Fig. 11

Pianoforte Steel wire
Normal temper

•

    From the Greek verb *hystereo*:

        I am late, I fall short, I lag behind.

In his 1885 paper, Sir Ewing framed it thus: *When there are two qualities M and N such that cyclic variations of N cause cyclic variations of M, then if the changes of M lag behind those of N, we may say that there is hysteresis in the relation of M to N.*

                                  : variations of a father on
a daughter and the daughter's changes to
herself   variations on the daughter charting how
her father changed herself   variations
of how a daughter struggles to erect a worthy image
of herself   lags behind
herself

It's not the truth you want—
it's the process,

walking back tonight, one foot
ahead of mine crossing traffic,
my husband says.

           Quick steps,
involuntary motions—
one moment, next, the way our lives
stitch into place behind us,
disappearing if we look.

Red light: a car stops, bass rumbling.
You're right, I say.
Though it's not enough.

                              •

                : either soft or glass-hard, cooled, annealed, taut or
                        normal-tempered, either steel or iron—

                saturate the wire with magnetic force, then chart its drop

•

        Tame is what he
        seems in this instant,
        chewing his beef in
        small efficient bites,

        eyes looking down
        at his dinner plate, those
        long black lashes my
        mother fell in love with
        fluttering thin.

        Old tiger prowling in
        a kinder, gentler cage:
        watched, he knows I'm
        watching him.

I want to tell you that it's beautiful—

one upward curve tracing the rise
in magnetic force, one plummeting

at precisely the same intervals, forming
a natural symmetry: a loop.

•

                Little things—
        pill bottles multiplying
        in his bedside tray. Hand
        against his back as
        he shuffles to the sink. Twitch
        of his white-socked foot
        as he nods off, TV blaring.

> I chat about the storm
> driving home tonight, where
> to shop tomorrow—
> placemats on the table, trivet
> beneath the bubbling dish—
> everyone is safe.
>
>   So I am cruel
> in this instant, an exploding
> bottle of ink—
> because I can't help thinking
> no *forgive and forget*, no *love
> always wins*.

> *Fig. 16*
>
> *Graded cyclical magnetisations
> of an Annealed Pianoforte Steel wire*

Let me tell you about *remanence*:

What remains of magnetism in the body
after the field has been removed.

We are talking, my sister and I, two feet
of distressed and varnished oak between us,
about our parents: how difficult our father's been,
where they'll retire, our paper cups of coffee
cooling off, my sister the doctor pleading,
*he's not going to change, I think
his neural pathways are set*, the tears
beginning to pool in her lovely eyes and I,
tearing up too, saying, *it's different for me, you see
I had a different experience with him.*

Though what I mean is I can't care
the way you do, I don't want to.

What remains (from the Latin *remanare*) varies with each material, but can be plotted as a point on the vertical H axis somewhere above the origin. Never zero: something always remains. Irrational, what remains.

•

> *Let's do it again*, I say to the cellist—
>
> rehearsing for a wedding, our notes
> brushing past each other's on the beat.
>
> Breathing in together, we start again,
> bows in unison: his eighths, my quarter.
>
> I could go on like this, I can practice forever
> when perfection is at stake, any emotion
>
> can be acted out regardless of how I feel,
> then placed to one side gently, framed,
>
> like a portrait hung beneath a light.

•

Oily: how his scalp smelled
on a humid summer evening,
neck of his white Hanes t-shirt
no longer actually white, cage

of his lips narrowing in anger,
buckling like a pencil tip pressed
too hard. I could do that to him.

Help him, help him, part of me still thinks.

"The value of M at any point of the operation depends not only on the actual value of N, but on all the preceding changes (and particularly on the immediately preceding changes) of N…"

                    I want to tell you that
                    it's beautiful, that beauty is more valuable
                    than truth since we can always manufacture
                    beauty, make beauty, even,
                    out of truth as well as lies and the loop
                    that forms between them,

                    I know there is no perfect
                    temperament, no perfect pitch: each note
                    on the piano borrows the shadow of its neighbor,
                    is the product of a host of strings
                    struck all at once. Every string exists
                    to be tightened, loosened, pushed.

                              •

Profiles—sheet after smooth, archival sheet in Sir Ewing's personal album—squiggled in black ink. Home in Edinburgh years after the hysteresis studies, after the team of cryptoanalysts he led during the Great War, he entertains his guests with a simple parlor game where each puts on a blindfold, pen in hand. Where the fun is watching the struggle to create. Pigs facing left. Pigs facing center. Curly tail, wiry tail, none. Joy in watching a hand not knowing where it's going, a black line emerge from nothing, swerve and carry on. Oh the risk of it, the laughter as the hand tears off the blind, the eye beholds what the body labored to trace. Lovable pigs; ugly pigs; comically distorted, under-realized pigs—no, not a true pig anywhere in the bunch. But the blossoming of ink across the waiting page, the serenity of space divided by these humble marks, pure pigs of the mind.

•

      : as in the dream where my father hands me
a beer, keeping a bottle for himself, and the trick is

do I take it, what does it mean to drink together
as we did—iced Cokes after he'd pummel me
with words, sometimes his fist? Now I drink
before I know what I am doing, taste how sharp
and clean it is, not like beer. I drink too fast—

I'll be drunk, I think, staring out the window.

•

I want to tell you that it's beautiful—

    all these moments felt in time

now graphed, side by side, so we can see that

    they were real, here were flames against this steel:

gas and blue and, no, the moments weren't

    beautiful, but sharp as flying gravel.

The loop remembers these, in this invented space

    where shape is memory, desire for

what could have been infinitely seen.

        Fig. 22

        Pianoforte Steel Wire
        Glass hard

Ghost

>   *—In the voice of Farinelli. London/Vienna/Rome, 1720s.*

Alone on the dressing room floor I sink,
back against the wall, wood beneath my feet.
I was good tonight.
                Good in all the roles
calling for heartbreak, peeling back the paper
from the fruit: like a moon, untouched. No one's left
but the man who will drive me home tonight,
wheels over cobblestone, lamps by the river. . .
supper laid with silver, Venetian crystal.
Sometimes a face appears between the flames—
my hands beneath the table open, close.

It's not that I can feel every heartbreak.
Each has a face that I create: ghost
in the stage light swirling, rising, smoke
for an instant.
             Until my raised hand drops,
my head bows and the house shakes with applause,
with pleasure—joy at the heart of heartbreak—
my feet bear me down the dark steps, backstage.
I am happy at this moment. Ravenous.

FOUR

Uses for Music

                        Because there is no soundtrack for the brain.

Because nothing has the beauty of a cage

                    you can enter when you want and leave behind.

So you can crawl across the floor and give it shape.
So one day you will release the snake—

                    you know, the one who lives inside you, has to move,
                    who can't keep still.

DEAR RICCARDO,

—Madrid. Winter, 1727.

                No time tonight to write
more than a scrap, dear Brother. You're correct:
I leave for Madrid tomorrow. All is settled.
I've barely touched ground since leaving the Court.
She had the wildest eyes, the Spanish Queen—
clutching my hand, whispering in my ear
so others near us couldn't hear, *You must come.*
Only the beauty of your voice can save Him.
Then tumbling from my lips, unaware, *Yes.*
I must be mad, Brother, as mad as he
to depart from this land for God knows what—
sitting here alone, all the dear old possessions
which made a life sinking into shadows.
I barely know the man writing these lines.

Your faithful CARLO

. . . .

                All you've heard about El Escorial—
colossal, bare, full of drafts and sackcloth—
is, I'm afraid, true. We have no comforts,
unless you count stone and iron comforts.
I've never climbed up a damper stairwell.
Thank God the Court's stay annual here
is brief. I can barely wait for winter,
when the whole palace flees to Aránjuez,
land of orange groves and plashing fountains.
It remains to be seen, Brother, what role
I create for myself at court. I have
my harpsichords, my books and paintings coming.
I can leave the palace at all hours
except when singing to the King. For now
that is enough. Picture me in good health

as I will picture you, walking every night
beneath the shade trees in Father's garden.
Send me the new aria you've written—
the one with the exiled prince in moonlight.

Give my best to Mother. Spare her details
you think would cause her suffering. My thoughts
and all my love I send across the ocean.

. . . .

A few lines more before I close this letter—
my nightly audience, you asked, how is he?
What can I say, Brother, in words alone?
He is a body crouched behind the curtains,
a hand mainly bones, the shuffle of linen.
He rasps and rocks and occasionally howls.
When he does, only an ancient servant,
one who nursed him as a boy, rushes in.
Only she can comfort him, good woman.
I do my part. What do you think I sing
but your own dear *Ombra fedele anch'io*?
"Faithful shade," indeed. I stand in darkness
by the foot of a bed enclosed by drapes
so thick I think of dark confession boxes,
imagine something worse. Curtains opened
only a hand's width: enough for one pair
of wolf's eyes, hungry, yellow in the flame.
I sing of love, of course, and ships and sailors
pining for the shore—my voice oddly still
my voice.

    There are nights when he barely breathes,
when his whole body strains to listen: I hear
his *silence*. And once, just once, after my last
held note, I heard his voice within the curtains—
Again. I want to hear that song again.

Your faithful CARLO

Eros the Hunter

You have the wet yellow eyes
of the dog who chased me.

           I was a child,
you had no mercy—
only hunger.

Spare me:
you are not yet human.
Or no longer.

. . .

You are the figure watching
from the root-tangled dirt
of a bed I want to drown
in daylight—

           you watch me
from the depths of,

           you wrought me.

But don't show me yet
those naked arms, don't flaunt your
purple wrists.

I will come to you
in my own time, lay my head against
your thumping chest.

Dear Riccardo, (II)

You must not think me miserable. No,
I am different here, I grow large and small
all at once, a curious bird to the ladies
who entreat me to sing. *My voice belongs
to my monarchs*, I say, bowing.

The Princess seeks me out:
she has no love for gloom, all for music.
Her music master—you will never guess—
Domenico, the son of old Scarlatti.
His hands are the fastest I've ever seen—
a wonder he has broken no instruments.
He plays like a tree being thrashed by a storm,
wet and blind, I mean. And yet he sings.

My deepest thanks again for Father's desk.
I can hardly tell you what joy it brings—
the old knobs and grooves; to open its drawers.
As I sit before it writing this letter
many hours run back to me: another life.
In both the old and the new, I remain,

Your devoted
CARLO

Everything Swims

—Farinelli and Scarlatti. Madrid, 1730s.

Too early for roses. Though even here—
where sunlight barely touches any windows,
the earth chokes with stones—every leaf turns green.

"You should find yourself better company,"
Scarlatti starts. "I'm not fit for the ladies, or,"
casting a sideways glance at me, "fine men."
Those eyes like a pair of keen medallions,
scarred but polished bright, flash across my body.
Hedges high and thick on both sides of us—
a thousand, ten thousand, shimmering leaves.
Shadows on the gravel: his footsteps, mine.

"You are a famous man. I do my best
to be no one." He kicks a stone in the air.

We both watch it rise then drop, invisible.
Time seems to flicker here, nearly blink.
"*Was* a famous man might be more correct."

"Obscurity protects us, don't you think?
Vulcan, Prometheus, etcetera—
they didn't meet the happiest of fates.
Here, in our little corner of the world,"
Scarlatti taps the boxwood as he walks,
"I thrive in the shadows like these hedges."

"There are many kinds of shadows, my friend."
What can I tell him of my nights? That fist
rapping the post with its blind, raw knuckles?

Taking off his hat, he wipes his forehead.
"I heard a tune in the street the other day so old
only the dead knew it. Sing it with me, *maestro*!"

Clapping his thigh, he hums something Gaelic,
wild, that only he would like, then turning,
slaps me heartily on the shoulder. I laugh.
What else can I do? I sing, picking out
a few, clear notes above his, that baritone
a cracked bronze bell, burnt sugar on the tongue.
The sun is climbing higher in the sky:
I remove my hat. Relentless, this spring.

•

"What do you remember about your father?"
Scarlatti's voice emerges from his chair.
Past midnight, portraits of the royal family
staring down at us from walls, candle-lit—
high, lonely faces, white as altar marbles.
I raise my glass to them in a silent toast.

"Everything strong and good, I suppose. Decent.
A loving husband, father, able composer.
And you? What made you think of this just now?"
"The same, of course. Oh, the man was perfect.
Imagine, his mind is a library, his hands"—
opening his, strong hands for octaves, tenths—
"two banks of the vast ocean. Inside them
everything swims, including you." He wipes his lips.

"Why, then, don't you want to write an opera?
You wrote many operas as a young man,"
I continue, leaning in, "like your father."

"And have you heard these fine works? Enough world,
my friend, exists already. Look around you.
Why create false ones with gods and heroes?
You were young, I think, when your father died?"

I slosh the wine in my glass. Strange how
separate a thing can feel, even in your hand.
You'll never be it. "Not so young."

"You premiered in London practically a child,
that I know. By twenty, I would guess, you'd made
all the money you could want from the stage."

I take a long sip. "Of the things he loved,
independence was what he loved the best.
My father wanted his sons to owe no one."

"Splendid. You've done exactly what he wished.
I suppose, dear *musico*, I am jealous.
I suppose I could have lived a different life,
spent my energies differently, not squandered—"
Lost in some reflection, he grows silent.

Soft

    Rain the whole drive home:
windshield wipers beating time
to *Die Fledermaus*.

    Fog. What you expect
in these mountains—not to see,
but move, anyway,

    forward like a bat
sensing higher frequencies
(or are they lower?)

    somewhere in its small,
unknowable body, soft
as ribboned velvet.

    And those words you read?
"But you should know that love is
also terrible."

    So when you realize
that you don't love your father,
what is *terrible*

    does not exist but
wants to, stretched like a drum
over something mute.

    The porch light greets you.
In the kitchen you release
the tap—cold water—

    fill the blue kettle,
fill your hands with bread, a knife.
That's when you hit it,

    slick beneath your heel,
something cool and small and wet.
Corner of a leaf?

    But when you nudge it,
something moves. Has a body
supple as a grape

    unpeeled, twin feelers
quivering in the dim air,
as if to taste it,

    softer than the leaves
that are dissolving into
ash outside your door.

    You can't forgive it.
Though how to say this danger—
why this simple slug

    should never exist,
why his need fills you with horror?
You can't just kill it.

    So scoop it quickly,
shuddering, into the trash,
where you will leave it

    masked beneath black mounds
of bitter coffee: one long,
bright reel of clementine.

Fire Chasing Air

    —Farinelli and Scarlatti. Madrid, 1740s.

"How immaculate your life seems to me."
Scarlatti stares at the white domed ceiling—
Orpheus sprawled against a grassy bank,
finger pointing grandly at the blank sky.

"The clean lines of your mind, its every wish,"
he nods at the pen in my hand, "transforming
into act. Never a doubt, not a wisp
of smoke in the chimney. A life like that—"
Scarlatti sinks into my couch, arms flung
across the slender mahogany back.

Laughing, I look up from my desk. Father's:
thick, blotted papers, some crinkling with heat.
I lay down my pen. The ink must dry.
He laughs, rubbing his eyes, staring out now
through the windows behind me at the park:
a still May morning, hedges half in shadow.

"How is the Scarlatti household these days?
The young Scarlattis and their mother well?"

"Yes, yes." Crossing to my table, he picks up,
puts down, first a Chinese fan, then a rock—
glass-smooth, black as a canal in Venice.
"How much pressure, do you think, did it take
to make this small stone smooth? How many years?
Fire chasing air. I used to think this thing, this
pressure, was desire. I was a young man.
It was all one soul chasing another—.
Then I thought it was my daimon: a voice
singing to me through the windows, late at night,
lovely in its own way, taunting me, of course."

He stares intently at the polished stone.
"A thing that's named can be called, can it not?
And if it's called, will it not come?"

Behind me I can hear the sounds of mowing,
swish of insect wings above high grass blades—
it's the time of year I love most, hate most,
when even the morning air swells with longing.
"*Sogno o vaneggio?*" I sing the line.

He looks at me, a little smile on his lips.
"Is it a 'dream' or a 'mirror'? . . . Indeed. *Orfeo*.
Memory serves you well, my friend.
Though you do not ask, nor do I tell you
what flits beneath the surface of this glass.
Perhaps," he turns the stone between his fingers,
"I fear to dent that smooth sail of your mind,
the singularity of purpose you enjoy from
a life so"—he pauses—"unconstrained."
I flinch. "Nothing is that simple."
I see the papers on my desk—all the same,
all the writing in my hand neat, ordained.

"Of course." He lays the stone back in its place,
tip of one finger hesitating still.
"I understand you paid my bills in town.
I did not dream—"

                    I wave my hand to stop him.
"Nothing should be owed between . . . true friends."

"I am grateful." Hands in his pockets now,
a sly smile pulls the corners of his mouth.
"My daimon thanks you, whatever his name."

BILDUNGSROMAN, 1999

—Tysons Corner, Virginia

It was late in the empire of concrete.
Vultures liked to perch on the austere ledge
outside my window, scouting the horizon.
Think of angels, then think their opposite:
all the things we ache to hide flung open,
soft, too soft, like a newborn barely formed.
They were cold, I think. Sun dried their feathers.
I was lonely, a head above a desk.
Ready to plunge into the glinting river
called the Beltway, below my office, catch
like a pebble in a wheel's stainless spokes.
This was before the towers fell. Before
the dot.com bubble burst, before Gitmo,
Dodd-Frank, Frodo in *The Lord of the Rings*.
All language to me then seemed violent,
all metaphor poignant, even suspect.
Driving to work: was that a metaphor?
Falling asleep on the couch work paid for,
stumbling toward the bed in my work clothes,
stripping in the dark, which was the old dark.
The man who was my tailor, a Korean—
I remember how he'd squat beside my feet,
pushing pins into the fabric here and there,
how he'd raise a stick of chalk, press firmly:
a hyphen, a hash mark snowy on the cloth.
How he'd pause to look up, from time to time,
and catch me standing still in his mirror,
the image of me staring at the mirror.
Everything is worth your look, I'd like to tell
that self, everything is still beautiful,
even if you have no words to say it.

To Hold Something Close

—Farinelli and Scarlatti. Aránjuez, 1740s.

"So she will *not* come here," speaks Scarlatti slowly.
"This woman who adores you, I can see,
whom you respect as you respect few people."
Back against an old beech tree, Scarlatti leans.
Behind us, men crossing the stage, hands full—
silk vines, screens painted with the moon and stars,
a pair of satin cloaks with ermine hems,
a long blue feather trailing from a hat.
"You must see that I'm not young anymore.
What you ask me to do is impossible."

"But you're not old, not by Nature's standards.
A ridge in this trunk"—he taps—"a sapling."

"Of all people, I thought you'd understand
what a man must do sometimes for freedom.
But the matter's done. I've sent my reply.
I would not have forced all of this on you—
you can't imagine how I hate it—but
I needed, wanted, to explain my silence."
Silver beneath the leaves, his eyes flicker.

"Dear *musico*, I've known you for too long—
I know how the walls of your building lean,
where the wind blows in, sun strikes its windows.
She won't come here because you refuse to be—"
he bends, plucking a fresh twig from the grass,
two or three green leaves still attached—"taken."

Reaching for my hand, he turns it palm-up,
lays the twig upon it, shuts my fingers.
"This is how it feels to hold something close."

Breaking Up with Eros

This morning, for example, I miss
your heat: how you flare my skin

into a sun, whipping my cold
dead planets into orbit. To slip

beyond the body's gate, glide
through its chain-link fence.

I need to find something beyond
just the physical—I've had enough from

Column A—proof you're more Apollo,
less *Saturn Devouring His Son*.

Mostly I want to be done with you.
Take a match to my fingers, grip

the shiny toilet with both hands, heave—.
Then it's night again. I'm out,

walking back after dinner, the air soft as
chalk on heavy paper, my pores

are open, ears open, I feel the bricks
of the courthouse crumbling, smell the ivy

crawling across them, bittersweet—
it's *you* I want again, your monstrous

light knocking my stained-glass window,
black ink of you raining swift down

parched map of me, blurring all my capitals.
That, at least, was irreparable.

FIVE

The Hydrangeas

All winter they curled like parchment, a band-aid
torn off in the shower, stiffening into final shape.

Because you believe that survival means
no one can teach you how to live, strength appears

gradually from suffering—you hurried past them.
Snow flung its iron cape over their heads.

Then one day, nearly April, all the little crocus pinged.
Death under such circumstances being out of place,

you fetched your clippers, crouched beside the bush.
What dropped into your bag was weightless.

•

Because to live we must forget—at least pretend—
they're back today as if nothing bad had happened,

blue as in the Quattrocento painting of a dying nymph,
where the mountain glides into a clear-bodied bay.

This early in the summer, there is nothing you can do.
They will become more and more themselves, intensify

in color, satisfy their simple wants through sun and rain.
Unlike us, their growing doesn't cast a shadow. Unlike

poetry, they feel nothing below their surface.
No one tells them, dimpling in the sun, *Remember this.*

•

They toss in the night like ghost ships—
fire on the ocean, flicker in the distance.

If you slipped out of bed, stole a glance
out your window, you would see
they are awake, they never sleep.

Pitching and tangling in the wind: one thing
never extinguishing the other.

•

This one, bent through the railings, could be your father.

He cries easily these days and naps in the afternoon.
She paints in the sunroom, easel toward the golf course.

And these two springing from one stalk, still green at the core—
your sister, you. Nights when you'd climb into her bed.

Behind them, petals overflowing like ruffles on the hem
of a sunbleached, ancient dress, stands your mother.
I'm not like the rest of you, you told her once.

She'd frowned then said, *I have faith you'll believe again.*

There are as many ways of knowing as desires to forget.

Floating on the water's surface, a thinker holding nothing,
a sculptor cutting stone to discover his own face,

the hands of a woman peeling orange after orange,
pith-pollened fingers that will never shake the terror
or the tenderness of naked flesh.

•

Because soon they will begin to fade.

Because, at the writing of this poem, they already have
        and you mourned them, lengthening your gaze.

Because we desire, always, to dissolve into
        something else, like clouds, shear,

as when you watch your father watch your mother,
        devoted as a dog begging to be fed.

Since what you truly love is distance, snow
        plump on car hoods, needles in the pines—

all the things that do not need you.

Because to clip them is a mercy, to plunge them
        into water, into an uncracked vase, the sum

of every gesture you have come to know as love.

•

                    Solstice: longest day of the year
lies down in the grass, nothing else to do.

Steaming, the colossal silver trout your friend caught
just this morning: gills crisping on the grill, belly slit
and stuffed with daylilies. Okra, summer squash, peaches

cut in half-moons transforming into something
beyond soft. *Watch out for the bones*, we say. So fine,
you could swallow one without regret.

Unfleshed, the rib cage gleaming on your plate,
like a dress without a woman: fluttering, weightless.

Post-

Clenching, unclenching her thin white fingers,
she tells me where the electric units sit.
Variable pulses, speed, duration—
dismantle what the body knows of trauma:

descending sheets of paper sheared
into ribbons. Harmless ribbons.

When a treatment "succeeds," the body goes dark.
As if birds had suddenly flown off a rooftop, birds
you hadn't noticed, wings threshing the air—

silence then, as if they'd never roosted there.

When I think about my father now, I feel nothing.

No, I'm like a rock with too many notches,
lichen growing silky as a coat across me, I'm the branch
that snapped last night during the wind storm.

Curved today across the trunk of my car—
whole, as if a hand had gently laid it there.

Bright Skin of a Snake

—Farinelli and Scarlatti. Aránjuez, 1750s.

"Your library is a model of order,"
I say, slipping off my gloves, folding them.
Walls of books, a few abandoned, tattered chairs,
one window propped half-open by a stick.
First breeze of summer evening drifting in.
The writing table where he sits, quickly copying,
fills most of the cluttered room, wood black,
all sides and corners—

"An octagon," he says, still scribbling.
"After the eight wind gods of ancient Greece.
Or some such. It's neither square nor circle,
though a little of both—that's what I like.
But I assume it's not your love of geometry
to which I owe the honor of this visit?"
He looks up at me, his eyes red and damp.

"The only wind I remember is Hebrides.
But no, I didn't come for geometry,
though I like this table: it suits you. No,"
I sit, choosing the chair closest to me,
"I haven't seen you all week. I feared you weren't well,
though Signora told me you are quite yourself."
I glance at the table: manuscripts, six,
seven piles arranged in stacks—fair copies.

"Myself." He smiles. "I am always myself.
Strange, don't you think, how much that little word
ropes off the world as we know it? As if,"
he leans back, looking up at the ceiling,
row after row of beams crossing the plaster,
"all our lives we ran only in parallel,
we never once pierced the skin of ourselves."
Laying down his pen, he rubs his eyes.

"So we *are* to speak of geometry?"
From the armrest one stray thread unfurls—
waving, colorless, mute. Easy to pull.
"Then I come to you, friend, as one of your
unpierced, parallel lives. Call me a line
marching forward since the day I left school—"
words tumble from my mouth, too quick, too much—
"I've taken pride in this—how shall I say?—
seamlessness. I am the infinite straight line.
And where has it brought me?"

Scarlatti leans back in his chair, shuts his eyes.
"When my father died, I was already forty.
Not a young man. I had been, as you've been,
wonderfully gifted with regularity.
With his death," he breathes deeply, "something fell,
dropped away—do you remember that tale?
Saul of Tarsus on the road to Damascus,
blinded by the mighty hand of God three days.
Once he believed, the Lord unblinded him."

He opens his own. "Then *something like scales*
fell from his eyes. That's how I felt. As if
in my hand lay the foiled bright skin of a snake,
newly sloughed, suddenly thin and weightless.
As if to say, you may now stop caring.
I say this because I have seen both sides—
life before and after that 'marching line'—
seen that I'm as likely to charm and disappoint
no matter what I say, what I do. You're different.
You're like a garden everyone goes to
for calm and beauty. You will always bloom."

Something like tears—no, actual tears—
fill my eyes, threaten to betray themselves.
"Odd to hear, since you don't care for gardens."
Out the window, the fields are growing dark.

"That's not true—it's not that I dislike gardens.
I dislike the life kept *out* of gardens,
all the weeds and overgrowth deemed unfit.
Though you're not one of those gardens, are you?"

I laugh. "If you mean that I am full of weeds,
you're correct. Though you surprise me, *maestro*,
to suggest that you are less than blooming."
I point to the papers beneath his pen.

"Oh, the sonatas!" He laughs or sighs. Both.
"Yes, they are a given. I must write them.
Not made for heavy burdens, as you know,
but I have no choice but to love them despite,
or *because* of, their lightness." He looks down.
"They are, anyhow, all that I have done."

We sit silent a moment. Night has come,
hay and wild honeysuckle threading the air.
Eventually he stirs himself and stands,
lights candles on the table, calls for wine.
I don't remember what we talked of next—
some long, amusing tale about his gardener
or the new French envoy—we talked, we drank.
I remember leaning back, head swimming,
thinking, *this, this, I will always want this.*

Another Sonata

You don't want to break.
And you do. Would. Even dream
how you will do it.

                                    Because the shape of
                   being human, I've begun
                   to think, is split.

Will transformation,
Rilke said. What did he mean?
(And do you want it?)

                                    Or like a fist,
                   opening and closing.
                   In "exposition," themes

                   are stated for the first
                   time. Exposed.

You love that freedom,

                                Like two hands spread
                   above piano keys.
                   Headphones jacked, I tap

                   my fingers to the beat.
                   Always wished I could play—

its open, colorless state—

                                a dream of unity?
                   Stepping into the forest,
                   feeling every leaf.

hate its shapelessness.

                        Two weeks away.
                        Tacking sheets
                        onto my corkboard:

                            sonatas by Scarlatti.
                        Trees outside my window.
                        Field. Birds. A cow.

So hard just to be.
Of course this is a cliché,
but look around you—

                            Five hundred fifty-five
                        sonatas by his death—black ink,
                        quick strokes,

                            hand copied
                        into red morocco notebooks.
                        Fifteen total.

these four walls, *your* walls,
dead ficus, books, end table.
So lightly acquired,

                        None of them followed
                        sonata form. None long: three,
                        maybe four minutes each.

                        Sunshine. Torrents.

the way lives are: yours.

                            In "development,"
                        themes wander through one

It overfills us,
Rilke writes. *We arrange it.*

It falls apart. We
rearrange it, and fall apart

ourselves. You wanted
to undo yourself, you didn't
want to break. You broke.

And the dream of how you did
shook you. Leaves you whole.

                    strange key after another,
                    time and space.

                    Home, I leave my suitcase
                    open for a week. Trees wave

                    outside my window—
                    the branches bend but

                    always snap in place.
                    (And the air, does it forget?)

                    In "recapitulation,"
                    the sonata brings us home.
                    Although the shape of

                    being human
                    shifts: departed from but
                    re-embraced. Like a cat

                                            walking home
                                    after a long disappearance,
                                    as if she'd never gone—

Like a freshly fallen twig.

                                    as if time left no trace—

Like a vase of cold water

                                    just the tip of one ear

spilling wide open.

                                    newly bitten.

Eros the Contagion

Soft as a Claude painting, the yellow sky tonight—
trees in the parking lot still thick, though the air, yes,
has an edge, the honey was solid in the jar
when I opened it this morning, found a single ant
frozen in the dunes, stunned by sweetness.
Can you really die of sweetness? Hard
to say yes, though I want to, looking up at these clouds
that make my heart jump: oh joy in seeing
though I can't touch, like the girl repeating *persimmon*
as the waitress in the diner tells her about a tree
at the top of the hill she used to climb, how beautiful
that vivid orange fruit was all at once.
Can't touch them, but I see them in her eyes as
she remembers persimmons. Maybe that was
my mistake: thinking every love was different, a fruit
inside its own clear mason jar—*my* love, *her* love, *his*,
all separate as the trees they fell from. Maybe love
is more contagion, bubbles in a bathtub slowly
swelling, all the little circles drifting, gliding
gently into each other until they burst, until
nothing's left but foam, the chime of rushing water.

Leap

He doesn't know about
your anger, glorious once
as December frost that vines
over windshields in the dark.

That once-love you jigsawed,
glued to cardboard, nailed
like a trophy to the wall.

This book.

How in its pages he becomes
the bridge you crossed to burn
more than a living father: yours.

O love like a beeswax,
like a skyscraper
you would leap from if you could,
from which all things come.

The Thief Dreams

To Hadrian's Wall

You were exactly what you seemed:
touchable, incapable of caring
about the ones you drove out, the ones
you kept in, or the guards who climbed your stones,
peering out at the black night so unlike
the Roman night, their heads pressed against
your unfeeling chest. You were a boundary.

Then you were a tail broken off
between the waving grasses, a toy
forgotten on a distant afternoon.
Red lines on a map. You'd been necessary
the way titles and bridges and collars
are necessary. Then you weren't.

Green in photographs today, your hillside.
Even your stones are picturesque;
crude, not perilous. What remains of danger
runs deep beneath the surface. What shines
from the open page has been curated.
In the dream I stand before you, eager,
lay my hand across your stones and look—
What remains?
              Miles of distant country,
green as only something past can be.
Or future. Where nothing will be finished,
no place left unseen.

Notes

About the real Domenico Scarlatti we know very little. Born in 1685 to that other famous Scarlatti (a prolific composer of opera and church music), Alessandro, Domenico Scarlatti married late, fathered numerous children, gambled frequently, and died relatively unknown in 1757. From 1729 until his death, he worked at the Spanish court as a music teacher to Princess Maria Barbara, writing sonata after sonata for the harpsichord. After her death, the 550+ sonatas he'd written became the property of his friend and court colleague for decades, Farinelli.

About Farinelli we know a bit more. Born Carlo Maria Michelangelo Nicola Broschi in 1705 to a composer father and castrated as a youth (like many Italian boys destined for singing careers at the time), he went on to become the most famous opera singer in Europe of his day. In 1737 he came to the Spanish court at the request of Queen Isabel Farnese to try a form of musical therapy on Philip V, singing nightly for the mad king, and becoming over time a close advisor to the Queen and director of the royal opera.

Ralph Kirkpatrick's *Domenico Scarlatti* (Princeton University Press, 1953) and Charles Burney's *The Present State of Music in France and Italy* (1773) provided source material for "Castrato," "Castrato ("desire must *vary*")," the "Dear Riccardo" letters, and the dialogues between Scarlatti and Farinelli. Kirkpatrick spent many years of his life performing Scarlatti sonatas on the harpsichord, cataloguing his work, and writing about his life and music.

"Violins: Violence" quotes a passage from the start of Book II of the *Meditations* by Marcus Aurelius, Gregory Hays's translation (Random House, 2002). "On the long way down/Oh oh oh oh oh oh" comes from Robert DeLong's 2015 song "Long Way Down."

"Castrato ("desire must *vary*")" quotes Roland Barthes's *S/Z: An Essay*, translated by Richard Miller (Farrar, Straus and Giroux, 1974).

"Girl Changing Shape" alludes to the myth of Mestra, daughter of Erysichthon the glutton, who acquired the power to change her shape at will after praying to her rapist, Neptune. I have quoted from Allen Mandelbaum's translation, *Metamorphoses of Ovid* (Harcourt, 1993).

"Soft" is a choka, an old Japanese form consisting of linked haiku. "But you should know that love is/also terrible" comes from C.G. Jung's *Liber Novus*, page 139, *Red Book: Liber Novus, A Reader's Edition* (W.W. Norton, 2009), as does the epigraph for the book.

"Breaking up with Eros" ends with a line by poet Frank Bidart from "In the Western Night," collected in *In the Western Night: Collected Poems, 1965-90* (Farrar, Straus and Giroux, 1990).

"Another Sonata" quotes poet Rainer Maria Rilke. "Will transformation" comes from Sonnet 12 of the "Sonnets to Orpheus," translated by Stephen Mitchell in *Ahead of All Parting: The Selected Poetry and Prose of Rainer Maria Rilke* (Random House, 1995). Lines from the "Eighth Elegy," translated by Edward Snow in *Duino Elegies* (North Point Press, 2000), appear later in the poem.

About the Author

Annie Kim is a poet, lawyer, and violinist. Her first book, *Into the Cyclorama* (2016), won the Michael Waters Poetry Prize and was a finalist for the *Foreword* INDIES Best Poetry Book of the Year. Kim's poems have appeared in journals such as *The Kenyon Review*, *Cincinnati Review*, *Beloit Poetry Journal*, and *Narrative*. She works as an assistant dean at the University of Virginia School of Law, teaches poetry and legal writing, and writes micro book reviews for *DMQ Review*.

Thanks

This book would never have completed the long road to print without the encouragement of many friends. I owe more to each of them than I can acknowledge:

To all my writer friends in the Warren Wilson MFA alumni community who inspire me daily, particularly to those who've pored over my manuscript at various stages of its life, whose sound advice, probing questions, and unwavering support kept me sane: Michael Collins, Marcia Pelletiere, Tracy Youngblom, and Jeff Talmadge.

To David Auerbach, Aaron Stepp, and Erika Howsare—friends and fellow artists—for staying true to their vision and helping me to stay true to mine.

To the friend who's known me the longest and still responds to my nonsense with love and wisdom, Melissa Levy.

To Andrea Carter Brown, whose bold editorial eye and intuition have strengthened this book in so many ways, and to Nancy White and all the writer/editors at The Word Works for their trust in this manuscript and their commitment to producing beautiful books.

To the Virginia Center for Creative Arts and the Hambidge Center for the Creative Arts and Sciences for the gift of weeks in the studio, where I produced many drafts and revisions that formed the backbone of this book.

And, finally, to my husband (who never wants to be acknowledged), for his daily jokes, uncompromising honesty, and unfailing love, without which I'd probably never write at all.

About The Word Works

Since its founding in 1974, The Word Works has steadily published volumes of contemporary poetry and presented public programs. Its imprints include The Washington Prize, The Tenth Gate Prize, The Hilary Tham Capital Collection, and International Editions.

Monthly, The Word Works offers free literary programs in the Café Muse series at the Writers Center in Bethesda, MD, and each summer it holds free poetry programs in Washington, D.C.'s Rock Creek Park. Word Works programs have included "In the Shadow of the Capitol," a symposium and archival project on the African American intellectual community in segregated Washington, D.C.; the Gunston Arts Center Poetry Series; the Poet Editor panel discussions at The Writer's Center; Master Class workshops; and a writing retreat in Tuscany, Italy.

As a 501(c)3 organization, The Word Works has received awards from the National Endowment for the Arts, the National Endowment for the Humanities, the D.C. Commission on the Arts & Humanities, the Witter Bynner Foundation, Poets & Writers, The Writer's Center, Bell Atlantic, the David G. Taft Foundation, and others, including many generous private patrons.

It is a member of the Community of Literary Magazines and Presses and its books are distributed by Small Press Distribution.

wordworksbooks.org

OTHER WORD WORKS BOOKS

Annik Adey-Babinski, *Okay Cool No Smoking Love Pony*
Karren L. Alenier, *Wandering on the Outside*
Karren L. Alenier, ed., *Whose Woods These Are*
Karren L. Alenier & Miles David Moore, eds.,
    Winners: A Retrospective of the Washington Prize
Christopher Bursk, ed., *Cool Fire*
Willa Carroll, *Nerve Chorus*
Grace Cavalieri, *Creature Comforts*
Abby Chew, *A Bear Approaches from the Sky*
Nadia Colburn, *The High Shelf*
Henry Crawford, *Binary Planet*
Barbara Goldberg, *Berta Broadfoot and Pepin the Short*
Akua Lezli Hope, *Them Gone*
Frannie Lindsay, *If Mercy*
Elaine Maggarrell, *The Madness of Chefs*
Marilyn McCabe, *Glass Factory*
Kevin McLellan, *Ornitheology*
JoAnne McFarland, *Identifying the Body*
Leslie McGrath, *Feminists Are Passing from Our Lives*
Ann Pelletier, *Letter That Never*
Ayaz Pirani, *Happy You Are Here*
W.T. Pfefferle, *My Coolest Shirt*
Jacklyn Potter, Dwaine Rieves, Gary Stein, eds.,
    Cabin Fever: Poets at Joaquin Miller's Cabin
Robert Sargent, *Aspects of a Southern Story*
    & *A Woman from Memphis*
Julia Story, *Spinster for Hire*
Miles Waggener, *Superstition Freeway*
Fritz Ward, *Tsunami Diorama*
Camille-Yvette Welsh, *The Four Ugliest Children in Christendom*
Amber West, *Hen & God*
Maceo Whitaker, *Narco Farm*
Nancy White, ed., *Word for Word*

THE WASHINGTON PRIZE

Nathalie Anderson, *Following Fred Astaire*, 1998
Michael Atkinson, *One Hundred Children Waiting for a Train*, 2001
Molly Bashaw, *The Whole Field Still Moving Inside It*, 2013
Carrie Bennett, *biography of water*, 2004
Peter Blair, *Last Heat*, 1999
John Bradley, *Love-in-Idleness: The Poetry of Roberto Zingarello*, 1995, 2ND edition 2014
Christopher Bursk, *The Way Water Rubs Stone*, 1988
Richard Carr, *Ace*, 2008
Jamison Crabtree, *Rel[AM]ent*, 2014
Jessica Cuello, *Hunt*, 2016
Barbara Duffey, *Simple Machines*, 2015
B. K. Fischer, *St. Rage's Vault*, 2012
Linda Lee Harper, *Toward Desire*, 1995
Ann Rae Jonas, *A Diamond Is Hard But Not Tough*, 1997
Annie Kim, *Eros, Unbroken*, 2019
Susan Lewis, *Zoom*, 2017
Frannie Lindsay, *Mayweed*, 2009
Richard Lyons, *Fleur Carnivore*, 2005
Elaine Magarrell, *Blameless Lives*, 1991
Fred Marchant, *Tipping Point*, 1993, 2ND edition 2013
Nils Michals, *Gembox*, 2018
Ron Mohring, *Survivable World*, 2003
Barbara Moore, *Farewell to the Body*, 1990
Brad Richard, *Motion Studies*, 2010
Jay Rogoff, *The Cutoff*, 1994
Prartho Sereno, *Call from Paris*, 2007, 2ND edition 2013
Enid Shomer, *Stalking the Florida Panther*, 1987
John Surowiecki, *The Hat City After Men Stopped Wearing Hats*, 2006
Miles Waggener, *Phoenix Suites*, 2002
Charlotte Warren, *Gandhi's Lap*, 2000
Mike White, *How to Make a Bird with Two Hands*, 2011
Nancy White, *Sun, Moon, Salt*, 1992, 2ND edition 2010
George Young, *Spinoza's Mouse*, 1996

THE HILARY THAM CAPITAL COLLECTION

Nathalie Anderson, *Stain*
Mel Belin, *Flesh That Was Chrysalis*
Carrie Bennett, *The Land Is a Painted Thing*
Doris Brody, *Judging the Distance*
Sarah Browning, *Whiskey in the Garden of Eden*
Grace Cavalieri, *Pinecrest Rest Haven*
Cheryl Clarke, *By My Precise Haircut*
Christopher Conlon, *Gilbert and Garbo in Love*
    & *Mary Falls: Requiem for Mrs. Surratt*
Donna Denizé, *Broken Like Job*
W. Perry Epes, *Nothing Happened*
David Eye, *Seed*
Bernadette Geyer, *The Scabbard of Her Throat*
Elizabeth Gross, *this body / that lightning show*
Barbara G. S. Hagerty, *Twinzilla*
Lisa Hase-Jackson, *Flint & Fire*
James Hopkins, *Eight Pale Women*
Donald Illich, *Chance Bodies*
Brandon Johnson, *Love's Skin*
Thomas March, *Aftermath*
Marilyn McCabe, *Perpetual Motion*
Judith McCombs, *The Habit of Fire*
James McEwen, *Snake Country*
Miles David Moore, *The Bears of Paris* & *Rollercoaster*
Kathi Morrison-Taylor, *By the Nest*
Tera Vale Ragan, *Reading the Ground*
Michael Shaffner, *The Good Opinion of Squirrels*
Maria Terrone, *The Bodies We Were Loaned*
Hilary Tham, *Bad Names for Women* & *Counting*
Barbara Ungar, *Charlotte Brontë, You Ruined My Life*
    & *Immortal Medusa*
Jonathan Vaile, *Blue Cowboy*
Rosemary Winslow, *Green Bodies*
Kathleen Winter, *Transformer*
Michele Wolf, *Immersion*
Joe Zealberg, *Covalence*

INTERNATIONAL EDITIONS

Kajal Ahmad (Alana Marie Levinson-LaBrosse, Mewan Nahro
       Said Sofi, and Darya Abdul-Karim Ali Najin, trans., with
       Barbara Goldberg), *Handful of Salt*
Liliana Ancalao (Seth Michelson, trans.), *Women of the Big Sky*
Keyne Cheshire (trans.), *Murder at Jagged Rock: A Tragedy by Sophocles*
Jeannette L. Clariond (Curtis Bauer, trans.), *Image of Absence*
Jean Cocteau (Mary-Sherman Willis, trans.), *Grace Notes*
Yoko Danno & James C. Hopkins, *The Blue Door*
Moshe Dor, Barbara Goldberg, Giora Leshem, eds., *The Stones
       Remember: Native Israeli Poets*
Moshe Dor (Barbara Goldberg, trans.), *Scorched by the Sun*
Laura Cesarco Eglin (Jesse Lee Kercheval and Catherine Jagoe,
       trans.), *Reborn in Ink*
Marko Pogačar (Andrea Jurjević, trans.), *Dead Letter Office*
Vladimir Levchev (Henry Taylor, trans.), *Black Book of the
       Endangered Species*

THE TENTH GATE PRIZE

Jennifer Barber, *Works on Paper*, 2015
Lisa Lewis, *Taxonomy of the Missing*, 2017
Brad Richard, *Parasite Kingdom*, 2018
Roger Sedarat, *Haji As Puppet*, 2016
Lisa Sewell, *Impossible Object*, 2014